KT-441-950

The Romantic Scotland of Kenneth McKellar

in picture and song

Ord and Loch Eishort, Isle of Skye.

Orchardton Tower, Kirkcudbrightshire.

The Romantic Scotland of Kenneth McKellar

in picture and song

Jarrold
Colour Publications

River Tweed and the Eildon Hills, Berwickshire.

85306 384 2
© 1972 Jarrold and Sons Limited, Norwich.
Printed and published in Great Britain by
Jarrold and Sons Limited, Norwich. 172.

Contents of this book

The great massif of Ben Nevis, Inverness-shire.

Foreword

Among the previous publications by Jarrold & Sons Limited, the beauty of Scotland has been warmly portrayed in the incomparable colour plates they have provided. Reflected in them has been a visual Scotland; a Scotland which endures in the minds of visitors and exiles alike, long after they have left its shores.

'Romance and novel', said Oliver Goldsmith, 'paint beauty in colours more charming than Nature and describe a happiness that man never tastes. How delusive, how destructive are those pictures of consummate bliss.'

Does a romantic Scotland then exist?

The camera does not lie! The history books do not lie – at least hardly ever!

Still with us in Scotland are the relics of a history so colourful and at times so bizarre as to stretch the imagination to its outer limits.

Still with us are the records of specific events written by men of the time, who in prose, poetry and music have brought the very stuff of history to life. Scotsmen have always, it seems, been ready to sit down and write honestly of their country; of its folk-lore, its history, its beauty, its enchantment, its *romance*! And we are fortunate in being not entirely dependent on their words for, even in the present day, we can experience with our own senses a Scotland so romantic as to occupy our thoughts and dreams for years to come.

My 'romantic' Scotland came to life when I was in my second year. The first word I spoke was 'Columba'. With such a start, I should have perhaps become a Christian missionary. However, I was apparently referring to the Clyde paddle-steamer named after 'The Apostle of Caledonia', which plied daily from Greenock to Ardrishaig on Loch Fyne. The Clyde and its islands were a second home to me at that time. Soon I came to identify the songs written around them, for most places of interest in Scotland have their *song*.

Beyond the Clyde to the west are the islands of the Hebrides with their quite distinct heritage of songs. Skye, Uist, Lewis, Mull, Mingulay, Eriskay, Jura, Islay and Barra all have their song! When the visitor leaves these islands, he takes the songs with him and he will find that they can evoke more warm memories than all his stock of colour-slides or guide-books

To the east of the Clyde is Ayrshire, the home of our National Poet, Robert Burns. His celebrity does not rest solely on the romantic. Even if it did, he would probably still have become our National Poet. His poems have a quality which tells of a spirit risen high above and beyond the fruitless furrow which he ploughed. His poem 'A Red Red Rose' is alone worthy of having blossomed on the Elysian Fields.

Before singing took up my whole interest, my profession was Forestry which I practised in various parts of Scotland. Traces of the original Caledonian Forest to be found here; fragments of song to be found there. The songs quickly became more absorbing than the trees.

'Loch Lomond' – its waters once ruffled by the keels of royal barges.

'The Royal Mile' – trodden by zealot and martyr; by triumphant Prince and fallen Queen.

'The Flowers of the Forest' – the flower of Scottish Chivalry, decimated on the field of Flodden.

'The Road to the Isles' – a colourful road to a destination as golden as Samarkand with songs to be gathered by the wayside.

These and many more places you will find among the following pages accompanying the songs. For it is through its songs, I feel, that you will realise another dimension to Scotland's beauty. And having realised this dimension, I hope you will return again and again to this book and to the country which it celebrates.

KENNETH McKELLAR

The Cairngorms from Boat of Garten, Inverness-shire.

Granny's Hieland Hame

M. MacFarlane

Chorus

Where the heather bells are blooming just outside Granny's door,
Where as laddies there we played in days of long ago,
Neath the shadow of Ben Bhragie and Golspie's loudly stane,
How I wished that I could see my Granny's Hieland hame.

Away in the Hieland
There stands a wee hoose,
And it stands on the breast of the brae,
Where we played as laddies
Sae long long ago,
And it seems it was just yesterday.

Where the heather bells are blooming, etc.

I can still see old Granny,
A smile on her face,
As sweet as the heather dew,
When she kissed me good-bye
Wi' a tear in her eye,
And said 'Laddie may God bless you.'

Where the heather bells are blooming, etc.

GRANNY'S HIELAND HAME
The 'Hieland hame' in the song is situated near Golspie in Sutherlandshire.

This was one of the many areas to suffer from the Highland Clearances in the nineteenth century. It is therefore not surprising that the evicted tenantry, exiled to Canada and elsewhere, should have constantly recalled with bitter longing the birthright they had been denied.

A piper by King Arthur's Seat, Edinburgh.

Scotland the Brave

C. Hanley

Hark when the night is falling,
Hear! Hear the pipes are calling,
Loudly and proudly calling,
Down thro' the glen.
There where the hills are sleeping,
Now feel the blood a-leaping,
High as the spirits of the old Highland men.

Towering in gallant fame,
Scotland my mountain hame,
High may your proud standards gloriously wave,
Land of my high endeavour,
Land of the shining river,
Land of my heart for ever,
Scotland the brave.

High in the misty Highlands,
Out by the purple islands,
Brave are the hearts that beat,
Beneath Scottish skies.
Wild are the winds to meet you,
Staunch are the friends that greet you,
Kind as the love that shines from fair maidens' eyes.

Towering in gallant fame, etc.

Additional verse

Far off in sunlit places,
Sad are the Scottish faces,
Yearning to feel the kiss
Of sweet Scottish rain.
Where tropic skies are beaming,
Love sets the heart a-dreaming,
Longing and dreaming for the homeland again.

Towering in gallant fame, etc.

Reproduced by kind permission of Kerr Music and Bayley & Ferguson Limited

SCOTLAND THE BRAVE
This song has become, in recent years, the veritable National Anthem of Scotland. The pipe-tune to which it is set is an old one.
The words, by Cliff Hanley, speak, like the man himself, straight from the heart.
The pipes can still be heard today 'loudly and proudly calling down through the glen'.

Wi' A Hundred Pipers

Lady Nairne

Wi' a hundred pipers an' a', an' a',
Wi' a hundred pipers an' a', an' a',
We'll up an' gie 'em a blaw, a blaw,
Wi' a hundred pipers an' a', an' a'.
O, it's owre the Border awa', awa',
It's owre the Border, awa', awa',
We'll on an' we'll march to Carlisle ha',
Wi' its yetts, its castle an a', an a'.

Wi' a hundred pipers an' a', an' a',
Wi' a hundred pipers an' a', an' a',
We'll up an' gie 'em a blaw, a blaw,
Wi' a hundred pipers an' a', an' a'.

Oh! our sodjer lads look'd braw, look'd braw,
Wi' their tartans, kilts, an' a', an' a',
Wi' their bonnets, an' feathers an' glitt'rin' gear,
An' pibrochs soundin' sweet and clear.
Will they a' return to their ain dear glen?
Will they a' return, oor Hieland men?
Second-sichted Sandy look'd fu' wae,
An' mithers grat when they march'd away.

Wi' a hundred pipers, etc.

O wha is foremaist o' a', o' a'?
O wha does follow the blaw, the blaw?
Bonnie Charlie, the king o' us a', hurrah!
Wi' his hundred pipers an' a', an' a'.
His bonnet and feather he's wavin' high,
His prancin' steed maist seems to fly,
The nor' wind plays wi' his curly hair,
While the pipers blaw wi' an unco flare.

Wi' a hundred pipers, etc.

The Esk was swollen, sae red, sae deep;
But shouther to shouther the brave lads keep;
Twa thousand swam owre to fell English ground,
An' danced themselves dry to the pibrochs' sound.
Dumfounder'd the English saw, they saw,
Dumfounder'd they heard the blaw, the blaw.
Dumfounder'd they ran awa', awa'.
Frae the hundred pipers an' a', an' a'.

Wi' a hundred pipers, etc.

Reproduced by kind permission of Bayley & Ferguson Limited

WI' A HUNDRED PIPERS
On 18 November 1745, the ancient city of Carlisle, after two days' show of resistance, opened its gates to Bonnie Prince Charlie. On entering the city the Prince was preceded by one hundred pipers.
The crossing of the River Esk, referred to in heroic terms, was, on the contrary, accomplished during the retreat from England in the concluding stages of the '45 Rising. However, the sight and sound of a hundred pipers playing this tune is stirring enough to fire any imagination and so perhaps Lady Nairne, who composed the song, can be forgiven her poetic licence.

Loch Creran lies between Loch Etive and Linnhe, Argyllshire

Mary of Argyll

C. Jeffries and S. Nelson

I have heard the mavis singing,
His love song to the morn;
I have seen the dew-drop clinging,
To the rose just newly born:
But a sweeter song has cheer'd me,
At the ev'ning's gentle close;
And I've seen an eye still brighter,
Than the dew-drop on the rose;
'Twas thy voice, my gentle Mary,
And thine artless winning smile,
That made this world an Eden,
Bonnie Mary of Argyll.

Tho' thy voice may lose its sweetness,
And thine eye its brightness too;
Tho' thy step may lack its fleetness,
And thy hair its sunny hue:
Still to me wilt thou be dearer,
Than all the world shall own;
I have loved thee for thy beauty,
But not for that alone;
I have watched thy heart, dear Mary,
And its goodness was the wile,
That has made thee mine for ever,
Bonnie Mary of Argyll.

Reproduced by kind permission of Kerr Music and Bayley & Ferguson Limited

MARY OF ARGYLL

The writers of both words and music were Englishmen: Charles Jeffries and Sydney Nelson. They wrote it about 1850.

It was no mean feat for them to compose a song which quickly came to be regarded by many – Scotsmen not excluded – as of equal rank to the songs of Burns himself.

Mary of Argyll has often been confused with the Mary, serenely statued near the pier at Dunoon in Argyll. She is, however, the 'Highland Mary', beloved of Burns in an earlier day.

The Bonnie Lass O' Ballochmyle

Robert Burns

Fair is the morn in flow'ry May,
  And sweet is night in autumn mild,
When roving thro' the garden gay,
  Or wand'ring in the lonely wild;
But woman nature's darling child:
  There all her charms she does compile;
E'en there her other works are foil'd,
E'en there her other works are foil'd
  By the bonnie lass o' Ballochmyle!

  The bonnie lass o' Ballochmyle,
  The bonnie lass!
  The bonnie, bonnie lass!
  The bonnie lass o' Ballochmyle.

O had she been a country maid,
  And I the happy country swain,
Tho' shelter'd in the lowest shed
  That ever rose on Scotland's plain!
Thro' weary winter's wind and rain,
  With joy, with rapture, I would toil;
And nightly to my bosom strain,
And nightly to my bosom strain
  The bonnie lass o' Ballochmyle.

  The bonnie lass o' Ballochmyle, etc.

Reproduced by kind permission of Bayley & Ferguson Limited

THE BONNIE LASS O' BALLOCHMYLE
Ballochmyle House stands on the banks of the River Ayr. In the time of Robert Burns, the house was occupied by Sir Claude Alexander, whose sister inspired the song.

In a letter to her, dated 18 November 1786, Burns described in lyrical and even passionate terms, the extent of her effect upon him and thus how the song had come to be written.

He never received a reply but in later years Miss Alexander freely acknowledged herself to be the lady in question and even had an arbour built on the spot where her path had crossed the poet's.

The musical setting commonly used nowadays is by William Jackson.

The Bluebells of Scotland

Mrs Grant of Laggan

Oh where and oh where is your Highland laddie gone?
Oh where and oh where is your Highland laddie gone?
He's gone to fight the foe for King George on the throne,
And it's oh! in my heart I wish him safe at home.

Oh where and oh where did your Highland laddie dwell?
Oh where and oh where did your Highland laddie dwell?
He dwelt in merry Scotland, at the Sign of the Blue Bell,
And it's oh! in my heart I love my laddie well.

Oh how, tell me how, is your Highland laddie clad?
Oh how, tell me how, is your Highland laddie clad?
His bonnet's of the Saxon green, his waistcoat of the plaid;
And it's oh! in my heart that I love that Highland lad.

Suppose, oh suppose that your Highland lad should die!
Suppose, oh suppose that your Highland lad should die!
The bagpipes should play o'er him, and I'd lay me down
  and cry;
But it's oh! in my heart that I feel he will not die.

Reproduced by kind permission of Kerr Music and Bayley & Ferguson Limited

THE BLUEBELLS OF SCOTLAND
Properly, 'The Bluebell of Scotland'. In most books of Scottish song, the air to which this song is sung is described as being of anonymous origin. However, on looking further into the matter, I find that the tune appears to have been of English origin, having had a place in The North Country Chorister *before it was known in Scotland.*

It was further noted as having been sung by a Mrs Jordan (an Irishwoman) at Drury Lane Theatre in London about 1801 under the title of 'Blue Bell of Tothill Fields' wherein the hero is a convict transported to Botany Bay.

The present words were written by a Mrs Grant of Laggan, Inverness-shire and refer to the Marquess of Huntly's departure for Holland with the British Forces under the command of Sir Ralph Abercromby in 1799.

River Nith near Ardoch, Dumfriesshire.

Liathach (3,456 feet) and Inner Loch Torridon, Ross and Cromarty.

My Heart's in the Highlands

Robert Burns

My heart's in the Highlands, my heart is not here;
My heart's in the Highlands, a-chasing the deer;
A-chasing the wild deer, and following the roe,
My heart's in the Highlands, wherever I go.

Farewell to the Highlands, farewell to the North,
The birthplace of valour, the country of worth;
Wherever I wander, wherever I rove,
The hills of the Highlands for ever I love.

Farewell to the mountains high covered wi' snow;
Farewell to the straths and green vallies below;
Farewell to the forests and wild-hanging woods;
Farewell to the torrents and loud-pouring floods.

My heart's in the Highlands, my heart is not here
My heart's in the Highlands a-chasing the deer;
A-chasing the wild deer and following the roe,
My heart's in the Highlands, wherever I go.

MY HEART'S IN THE HIGHLANDS
This song was probably charmed out of Burns by recollections of his third and last tour in the North in 1787.

Of the words of the song Burns wrote: 'The first half-stanza of this song is old, the rest is mine; and there exists some doubt as to whether these four lines belong to a Scotch or an Irish source, the pros and cons being pretty evenly balanced.'

The air is an old Highland one.

The delightful gardens below Edinburgh Castle.

The Bonnie Wells O' Wearie

A. Maclagan and J. C. Grieve

Come let us climb Auld Arthur Seat,
When summer flowers are blooming;
When golden broom and heather bells
Are a' the air perfuming,
When sweet May gowans deck the braes,
The hours flee fast fu' cheerie,
Where bonnie lasses bleach their claes
Beside the Wells o' Wearie.

The bonnie Wells o' Wearie!
The bonnie Wells o' Wearie!
Come, let us spend a summer day
Beside the Wells o' Wearie.

There Scotland's Queen in stormy times
Forgot her saddest story;
There brave Prince Charlie led his clans
To deeds o' martial glory.
When Johnnie Cope wi' a' his men
Were scattered tapselteerie,
There Scotland's banner proudly wavéd
Beside the Wells o' Wearie.

The bonnie Wells o' Wearie!, etc.

Then let us hail Auld Arthur Seat;
Like Scotland's Rampant Lion,
It towers a wonder o' the world,
The wildest storms defying.
Wi' dauntless front neath summer skies
Or wintry blasts sae dreary,
It stands, in peace or war to guard
The bonnie Wells o' Wearie.

The bonnie Wells o' Wearie!, etc.

Reproduced by kind permission of Kerr Music and Bayley & Ferguson Limited

THE BONNIE WELLS O' WEARIE
The Wells o' Wearie are situated at the southern bend of the Queen's Park in Edinburgh, not far from the foot of Arthur's Seat.

The writer of the words was one Alexander Maclagan who was born in Perth in 1811 and who combined the occupation of poet with that of a plumber.

The melody was written by John Charles Grieve, born in Edinburgh in 1842 and perhaps best known as the inaugurator of the kinderspiel *– a kind of children's opera.*

Scots Wha Hae

Robert Burns

Scots, wha hae wi' Wallace bled,
Scots, wham Bruce has often led,
Welcome to your gory bed,
Or to victorie!

Now's the day, and now's the hour;
See the front o' battle lour,
See approach proud Edward's pow'r –
Chains and slaverie!

Wha will be a traitor knave?
Wha can fill a coward's grave?
Wha sae base as be a slave?
Let him turn and flee!

Wha for Scotland's King and law
Freedom's sword will strongly draw?
Freeman stand, or freeman fa'?
Let him follow me!

By oppression's woes and pains!
By your sons in servile chains!
We will drain our dearest veins,
But they shall be free!

Lay the proud usurper low!
Tyrants fall in ev'ry foe!
Liberty's in ev'ry blow!
Let us do or die!

Reproduced by kind permission of Kerr Music and Bayley & Ferguson Limited

SCOTS WHA HAE
The words, written by Burns, were entitled 'Address of Bruce to his Troops' and delivered to his friend Mr Syme on 2 August 1793. It recalls the confrontation between the army of Bruce and that of Edward II at Bannockburn in the summer of 1314. It was under Bruce's leadership that Scotland regained her freedom.

The twenty-foot-high mounted statue of Bruce, sculpted by Pilkington Jackson and set up at Bannockburn in 1964, does great justice to the heroic leader of the Scots and to their glorious day which inspired Burns to write these words.

The Bonnie Banks of Loch Lomond.

Loch Lomond

Anonymous

By yon bonnie banks and by yon bonnie braes,
Where the sun shines bright on Loch Lomond,
Where me and my true love were ever wont to gae,
On the bonnie, bonnie banks of Loch Lomond.

O, ye'll tak' the high road an' I'll tak' the low road,
An' I'll be in Scotland afore ye,
But me an' my true love will never meet again
On the bonnie, bonnie banks of Loch Lomond.

I mind when we parted in yon shady glen,
On the steep, steep side of Ben Lomond,
Where in purple hue the Highland hills we view,
And the moon looks out from the gloamin'.

O, ye'll tak' the high road, etc.

Reproduced by kind permission of Kerr Music and Bayley & Ferguson Limited

LOCH LOMOND
Lady John Scott (1810–1900) and her husband 'picked up' both verses and melody 'from a poor boy in the streets of Edinburgh'. It had been almost certainly composed in 1745 but was not published until about 1845.

In 1745, Bonnie Prince Charlie was in retreat from England and some of his wounded had to be left behind in Carlisle. The song refers to two of them, one to be released and the other to be executed at the same hour.

According to Celtic belief, the spirit of the dead prisoner travelling by the 'low road' back to his birthplace would reach Scotland before his comrade who would have to trudge many miles there by the 'high road' of the living.

Bonnie Strathyre

Sir Harold Boulton

There's meadows in Lanark and mountains in Skye,
And pastures in Hielands and Lowlands foreby,
But there's nae greater luck that the heart could desire,
Than to herd the fine cattle in Bonnie Strathyre.

Oh, it's up in the morn and awa' to the hill,
Where the lang summer days are sae warm and sae still,
Till the peak of Ben Vorlich is girdled with fire,
And the evening falls gently on Bonnie Strathyre.

Then there's mirth in the sheiling and love in my breast,
When the sun is gaen doon and the kye are at rest,
For there's mony a prince would be proud to aspire,
To my winsome wee Maggie the pride of Strathyre.

Oh her lips are like rowans in ripe summer seen,
And mild as the starlight the glint 'o her een,
How sweet is her breath as scent o' the brier,
And her voice is sweet music in Bonnie Strathyre.

Set Flora by Colin and Maggie by me,
And we'll dance to the pipes swelling loudly and free,
Till the moon in the heavens climbing higher and higher,
Bids us sleep on fresh brackens in Bonnie Strathyre.

Though some in the toons o' the Lowlands seek fame,
An' some would gang soldiering far frae their hame,
Yet I'll ay herd my cattle and bigg my ain byre,
And love my ain Maggie in Bonnie Strathyre.

BONNIE STRATHYRE
The Valley of Strathyre lies in 'Lady of the Lake' country between Callander and Lochearnhead in Perthshire.

It continues to hold its place among the many favourite holiday places in Scotland.

Ben Vorlich (3,224 feet) looks down over the village and climbers who don't wish to be too ambitious can scramble to their hearts' content on the pretty slopes of the Ben of the Fairies.

The words of this song were written by Sir Harold Boulton and set by him to the adapted traditional air, 'Taymouth'.

Loch na Garr

Lord Byron

Away, ye gay landscapes, ye gardens of roses,
  In you let the minions of luxury rove;
Restore me the rocks where the snow-flake reposes,
  Though still they are sacred to freedom and love:
Yet Caledonia, beloved are thy mountains,
  Round their white summits though elements war;
Though cataracts foam 'stead of smooth-flowing fountains,
  I sigh for the valley of dark Loch na Garr.

Ah! there my young footsteps in infancy wander'd;
  My cap was the bonnet, my cloak was the plaid;
On chieftains long perish'd my memory ponder'd,
  As daily I strode through the pine-cover'd glade;
I sought not my home till the day's dying glory
  Gave place to the rays of the bright polar star;
For fancy was cheer'd by traditional story,
  Disclos'd by the natives of dark Loch na Garr.

'Shades of the dead! have I not heard your voices
  Rise on the night-rolling breath of the gale?'
Surely the soul of the hero rejoices
  And rides on the wind o'er his own Highland vale.
Round Loch na Garr, while the stormy mist gathers,
  Winter presides in his cold icy car:
Clouds there encircle the forms of my fathers;
  They dwell in the tempests of dark Loch na Garr.

'Ill-starr'd, though brave, did no visions foreboding
  Tell you that fate had forsaken your cause?'
Ah! were you destin'd to die at Culloden,
  Victory crown'd not your fall with applause:
Still were you happy in death's earthly slumber,
  You rest with your clan in the caves of Braemar;
The pibroch resounds to the piper's loud number,
  Your deeds on the echoes of dark Loch na Garr.

Years have roll'd on, Loch na Garr, since I left you,
  Years must elapse ere I tread you again:
Nature of verdure and flowers has bereft you,
  Yet still are you dearer than Albion's plain.
England! thy beauties are tame and domestic
  To one who has roved o'er the mountains afar:
Oh for the crags that are wild and majestic!
  The steep frowning glories of dark Loch na Garr.

Reproduced by kind permission of Kerr Music and Bayley & Ferguson Limited

LOCH NA GARR
The poem is by Lord Byron and was included in his Hours of Idleness *(1807). Byron spent part of his early life near Loch na Garr, which, together with Ben Macdhui, Cairntoul and Cairngorm, from the Cairngorm range of mountains, rising at the meeting of the Shires of Inverness, Banff and Aberdeen. Its height is approximately 3,777 feet.*

Byron described Loch na Garr as 'certainly one of the most sublime and picturesque among our Caledonian Alps'.

The air was composed by an Edinburgh lady, Mrs Patrick Gibson (1786–1838) who, apart from keeping a boarding-school for ladies in Inverleith Row, also displayed in her setting what I presume to be a mischievous approach to the range of the tenor voice!

Sunset over Schiehallion and Loch Tummel, Perthshire.

Beautiful Loch Achray.

Land O' Heart's Desire

Marjory Kennedy-Fraser

Land o' Heart's Desire,
Isle of Youth,
Dear Western Isle,
Gleaming in sunlight!
Land o' Heart's Desire,
Isle of Youth!

Far the cloudless sky
Stretches blue
Across the Isle,
Green in the sunlight,
Far the cloudless sky
Stretches blue.

There shall thou and I
Wander free,
On sheen-white sands,
Dreaming in starlight,
Land o' Heart's Desire,
Isle of Youth.

Reprinted from Songs of the Hebrides *by permission of the Trustees of the Estate of Marjory Kennedy-Fraser and Boosey & Hawkes, Music Publishers Limited*

LAND O' HEART'S DESIRE
Since long before the stormy Western seas were first laid open by the keel of a ship, the souls of the Celtic people have longed for immortality in a land of their own choosing.

That it is to be a land of eternal sunshine is natural to the Celtic race but that it should be also a land of eternal freedom is the hope of all mankind.

The English words here given are by Marjory Kennedy-Fraser and the melody to which they are sung was collected in North Uist.

The peaceful River Stinchar at Colmonell, Ayrshire.

Ye Banks and Braes

Robert Burns

Ye banks and braes o' bonnie Doon,
  How can ye bloom sae fresh and fair?
How can ye chant ye little birds,
  And I sae weary, fu' o' care?
Ye'll break my heart, ye warbling birds,
  That wanton through the flow'ry thorn,
Ye mind me o' departed joys,
  Departed never to return.

Oft hae I rov'd by bonnie Doon,
  To see the rose and woodbine twine;
And ilka bird sang o' its love,
  And fondly sae did I o' mine.
Wi' lightsome heart I pu'd a rose,
  Fu' sweet upon its thorny tree;
And my fause lover stole my rose,
  But ah! he left the thorn wi' me.

Reproduced by kind permission of Bayley & Ferguson Limited

YE BANKS AND BRAES
This song by Robert Burns commemorates the hapless love of a young Ayrshire girl who fell victim to the faithlessness of a local laird. 'Most bitter sorrow shrined in strain most sweet.'

The River Doon flows near by the birthplace of Burns at Alloway and it was over this same river that Tam o' Shanter was chased by 'Cutty Sark' and her fellow witches.

Afton Water

Robert Burns

Flow gently, sweet Afton, among thy green braes,
Flow gently, I'll sing thee a song in thy praise;
My Mary's asleep by thy murmuring stream;
Flow gently, sweet Afton, disturb not her dream.

Thou stock-dove, whose echo resounds thro' the glen,
Ye wild whistling blackbirds in yon thorny den,
Thou green-crested lapwing thy screaming forbear,
I charge you disturb not my slumbering fair.

How lofty, sweet Afton, thy neighbouring hills,
Far mark'd with the courses of clear winding rills;
There daily I wander as noon rises high,
My flocks and my Mary's sweet cot in my eye.

How pleasant thy banks and green valleys below,
Where wild in the woodlands the primroses blow;
There oft as mild ev'ning creeps over the lea,
The sweet-scented birk shades my Mary and me.

Thy crystal stream, Afton, how lovely it glides,
And winds by the cot where my Mary resides;
How wanton thy waters her snowy feet lave,
As gathering sweet flow'rets she stems thy clear wave!

Flow gently, sweet Afton, among thy green braes,
Flow gently, sweet river, the theme of my lays:
My Mary asleep by thy murmuring stream,
Flow gently, sweet Afton, disturb not her dream.

Reproduced by kind permission of Kerr Music and Bayley & Ferguson Limited

AFTON WATER
This Burns's song was presented by the poet to Mrs General Stewart of Stair and Afton, who was the first lady of 'station' to realise his genius. It later appeared in James Johnson's The Scots Musical Museum *in 1792.*

In 1786 when the song was written, Burns was in love with Mary Campbell ('Highland Mary') and it is to be supposed that she is the 'Mary' referred to in the song.

The Afton is a small Ayrshire tributary of the River Nith running through what was once the property of Mrs General Stewart who is reported to have been 'extremely gratified by the poet's reference to her domain'.

Kilchurn Castle, on Loch Awe, Argyllshire.

MacGregor's Gathering

Sir Walter Scott

The moon's on the lake, and the mist's on the brae,
And the clan has a name that is nameless by day;
Then gather, gather, gather, Grigalach!
Gather, gather, gather, etc.

Our signal for fight, that from monarchs we drew,
Must be heard but by night in our vengeful haloo!
Then haloo, Grigalach! haloo, Grigalach!
Haloo, haloo, haloo, Grigalach, etc.

Glen Orchy's proud mountains, Coalchuirn and her towers,
Glenstrae and Glenlyon no longer are ours;
We're landless, landless, landless, Grigalach!
Landless, landless, landless, etc.

But doom'd and devoted by vassal and lord,
MacGregor has still both his heart and his sword!
Then courage, courage, courage, Grigalach!
Courage, courage, courage, etc.

If they rob us of hame, and pursue us with beagles
Give their roofs to the flame, and their flesh to the eagles!
Then vengeance, vengeance, vengeance, Grigalach!
Vengeance, vengeance, vengeance, etc.

While there's leaves in the forest, and foam on the river,
MacGregor, despite them, shall flourish for ever!
Come then, Grigalach, come then, Grigalach,
Come then, come then, come then, etc.

Through the depths of Loch Katrine the steed shall career,
O'er the peak of Ben Lomond the galley shall steer,
And the rocks of Craig-Royston like icicles melt,
Ere our wrongs be forgot, or our vengeance unfelt!
Then gather, gather, gather, Grigalach!
Gather, gather, gather, etc.

MACGREGOR'S GATHERING
By an act of the Privy Council, dated 3 April 1603, the name of Macgregor was expressly abolished and those who had borne it were commanded to change it for other surnames on pain of death. By a subsequent Act of Council on 24 June 1613, death was pronounced against members of the Macgregor Clan presuming to assemble in numbers greater than four.

This lyric on the subject was written by Sir Walter Scott and contributed by him to Albyn's Anthology *in 1816.*

Glen Orchy lies in Argyllshire between Loch Awe and Perthshire.

The ruined castle of 'Coalchuirn' stands at the eastern end of Loch Awe.

Glenstrae is the valley which opens on to Loch Awe.

Glenlyon is a long narrow valley in the north-west of Perthshire.

Loch Katrine lies in the Trossachs and 'Craig-Royston' is a cave on the western side of Ben Lomond.

The melody to which the lyric is set was composed by Alexander Lee, a popular singer who was born in London in 1802 where he died forty-nine years later.

Glen Trool, Kirkcudbrightshire.

The Rowan Tree

Lady Nairne

O rowan tree, O rowan tree! thou'lt aye be dear to me;
Entwin'd thou art wi' mony ties o' hame and infancy.
Thy leaves were aye the first o' spring,
Thy flow'rs the simmer's pride,
There was nae sic a bonny tree in a' the countrie side.
O rowan tree.

How fair wert thou in simmer time, wi' a' thy clusters white,
How rich and gay thy autumn dress, wi' berries red and bright.
On thy fair stem were mony names, which now nae mair can I see,
But they're engraven on my heart – forget they ne'er can be.
O rowan tree.

We sat aneath thy spreading shade, the bairnies round thee ran,
They pu'd thy bonnie berries red, and necklaces they strang.
My mother! Oh! I see her still, she smil'd our sports to see,
Wi' little Jeanie on her lap, and Jamie at her knee!
O rowan tree.

Oh! there arose my father's prayer in holy evening's calm,
How sweet was then my mother's voice in the Martyr's psalm;
Now a' are gane! we meet nae mair aneath the rowan tree;
But hallowed thoughts around thee turn o' hame and infancy.
O rowan tree.

Reproduced by kind permission of Bayley & Ferguson Limited

THE ROWAN TREE
In Scotland at one time there was hardly a home of any kind which did not have a rowan tree growing near by.

The Rowan or Mountain Ash was able to ward off evil in any form, were it 'bogles' or the Legions of Hell themselves. In consequence of this, the rowan was omnipresent in memories of childhood, whether spent in bothy or castle.

Lady Nairne wrote these words which recall the most tender scenes of early days.

Annie Laurie

Lady Scott

Maxwellton braes are bonnie
Where early fa's the dew,
And 'twas there that Annie Laurie
Gave me her promise true,
Gave me her promise true;
Which ne'er forgot will be,
And for bonnie Annie Laurie
I lay me doon and dee.

Her brow is like the snowdrift,
Her throat is like a swan,
Her face it is the fairest
That e'er the sun shone on;
That e'er the sun shone on,
And dark blue is her ee,
And for bonnie Annie Laurie
I lay me doon and dee.

Like dew on th' gowan lying
Is th' fa' o' her fairy feet,
And like winds in summer sighing
Her voice is low and sweet,
Her voice is low and sweet,
And she's a' the world to me,
And for bonnie Annie Laurie
I lay me doon and dee.

Reproduced by kind permission of Kerr Music and Bayley & Ferguson Limited

ANNIE LAURIE
This well-known melody was written by Lady John Scott (1810–1900), who also altered the second verse from an earlier original and composed the third verse. It was popular with the British troops during the Crimean War.

In spite of popular belief, the Annie Laurie who lies buried in Glencairn Churchyard in Dumfriesshire, near the 'bonnie braes of Maxwellton', was not the lady about whom the song was originally written. A romantic story was woven round her name but, alas, like many romances, it was based less on fact than on fancy.

St Mary's Loch, Selkirkshire.

O My Love is Like a Red Red Rose

Robert Burns

O my love is like a red red rose,
That's newly sprung in June:
O my love is like a melodie,
That's sweetly play'd in tune.
As fair art thou, my bonnie lass,
So deep in love am I:
And I will love thee still, my dear,
Till a' the seas gang dry.

Till a' the seas gang dry, my dear,
Till a' the seas gang dry,
And I will love thee still my dear,
Till a' the seas run dry.

Till a' the seas gang dry, my dear,
And the rocks melt wi' the sun,
And I will love thee still, my dear,
While the sands o' life shall run.
And fare thee weel, my only love,
And fare thee weel awhile!
And I will come again, my love
Tho' 'twere ten thousand mile.

Tho' 'twere ten thousand mile, my love,
Tho' 'twere ten thousand mile,
And I will come again, my love,
Tho' 'twere ten thousand mile.

Reproduced by kind permission of Kerr Music and Bayley & Ferguson Limited

O MY LOVE IS LIKE A RED RED ROSE
'Rough ore, thrown into the melting-pot of Robert Burns' genius, comes out as purest gold.'

The present song is made up of three old ballads which Burns adapted and had published in James Johnson's The Scots Musical Museum. *Three tunes have been associated with it; first, 'Major Graham' and then 'Queen Mary's Lament' but later, the melody to which it is now sung became the most popular – it is called 'Low Down in the Broom'.*

The Long Ships

E. Boyd and K. McKellar

Bend of arm and swing of shoulder
Cold the wind, but death is colder,
Hee-o ho! Hee-o ho! Hee-o ho!

Blow of spume and crash of breaker
Ho! Sword the orphan-maker,
Hee-o ho! Hee-o ho! Hee-o ho!

Bright the oar, the billow reaping
On the shore, the women weeping,
Hee-o ho! Hee-o ho! Hee-o ho!

Bend of keel, the land before us,
Thor and Odin hear our chorus,
Hee-o ho! Hee-o ho!
Hear our chorus, Hee-o ho! Hee-o ho!

Reprinted by permission of Boosey & Hawkes, Music Publishers Limited

THE LONG SHIPS
This song was written by Eddie Boyd and myself during a film we were making for the B.B.C. in the Outer Hebrides.
The seas around the Hebrides were once the scene of savage battles between the longships of the Vikings and the boats of the islanders.
Those longships were built for speed and the men who drove them forward were built and trained for warfare.
On seeing a raging sea thundering against the Hebridean cliffs, one can begin to visualise these men who showed mercy to none.

The Isle of Mull

Dugald MacPhail (translated by Malcolm MacFarlane)

Chorus

The Isle of Mull is of the Isles the fairest,
Of ocean's gems 'tis the first and rarest;
Green grassy island of sparkling fountains,
Of waving woods and high tow'ring mountains.
Tho' far from home, I am now a ranger,
In grim Newcastle a doleful stranger;
The thought of thee stirs my heart's emotion,
And deeper fixes its fond devotion.

Oh! fresh and fair are thy meadows blooming,
With fragrant blossoms the air perfuming;
Where boyhood days I've oft spent in fooling
Around Ben Varnick and Durry Cooling.

The Isle of Mull, etc.

Where Lussa's stream thro' the pools comes whirling,
Or o'er the clear pebbly shallows swirling;
The silv'ry salmon is there seen playing,
And in the sunbeams his hues displaying.

The Isle of Mull, etc.

There might young manhood find fit enjoyment,
In healthy, vigorous, rare employment;
With three-pronged spear on the margin standing,
And with quick dart the bright salmon landing.

The Isle of Mull, etc.

How pleasant 'twas in the sweet May morning,
The rising sun thy gay fields adorning;
The feather'd songsters their lays were singing,
While rocks and woods were with echoes ringing.

The Isle of Mull, etc.

But gone are now all those joys for ever,
Like bubbles bursting on yonder river;
Farewell, farewell, to thy sparkling fountains,
Thy waving woods and high tow'ring mountains.

The Isle of Mull, etc.

THE ISLE OF MULL
The island of Mull is the largest of the Inner Hebrides and perhaps the richest in variety of scenery and interest. Like a mother hen surrounded by her chicks, Mull has around her many smaller islands of great interest, among them Iona, Staffa, Ulva, Gometra and Inch Kenneth.
The song is one of longing in exile – in this case in 'grim Newcastle'.
The air is traditional Gaelic and the translation into English was done by Malcolm MacFarlane.

Sunset from Tobermory, Isle of Mull.

Tranquil Gruinard Bay, Ross and Cromarty.

Kishmul's Galley

Mrs MacLean of Barra

High from the Ben a Hayich,
On a day of days
Seaward I gazed,
Watching Kishmul's galley sailing.

Homeward she bravely battles
'Gainst the hurtling waves,
Nor hoop nor yards,
Anchor, cable nor tackle has she.

Now at last, 'gainst wind and tide,
They've brought her to
Neath Kishmul's walls,
Kishmul Castle, our ancient glory.

Here's red wine and feast for heroes
And harping too,
Sweet harping too.

Reprinted from Songs of the Hebrides *by permission of the Trustees of the Estate of Marjory Kennedy-Fraser and Boosey & Hawkes, Music Publishers Limited*

KISHMUL'S GALLEY
The castle of Kishmul or Kisimul stands on a little island-rock in Castle Bay in the island of Barra.

The castle of a thousand years ago possessed a war galley similar to the Norse design and usually carrying a crew of sixty-four. It was used to defend the castle and to sail on expeditions of plunder among the other islands of the Hebrides, to Ireland and to the Mainland of Scotland.

The return of the galley to the friendly shores of Barra is commemorated in the song by a lookout on the slopes behind Castle Bay.

The words are from Mrs MacLean of Barra and the air was taken down from the singing of Mary Macdonald of Mingulay.

View from Bridge of Crudie, Ross and Cromarty.

Westering Home

Sir Hugh Roberton

Chorus

And it's Westering home, and a song in the air,
Light in the eye, and it's good-bye to care;
Laughter o' love, and a welcoming there;
Isle of my heart, my own one!

Tell me o' lands o' the Orient gay!
Speak o' the riches and joys o' Cathay!
Eh, but it's grand to be wakin' ilk day
To find yourself nearer to Isla.

And it's Westering home, and a song in the air, etc.

Where are the folk like the folk o' the west?
Canty, and couthy, and kindly, the best;
There I would hie me and there I would rest
At hame wi' my ain folk in Isla.

And it's Westering home, and a song in the air, etc.

Reproduced by kind permission of Roberton Publications

WESTERING HOME
A song bubbling with joy at the prospect of a homecoming to the islands of the West.

The words are by Sir Hugh Roberton who was conductor of the famous Glasgow Orpheus Choir and a devotee of all that was best in Scotland.

Coming as I do from the West of Scotland, I don't know that I could disagree with anything he says in the song.

The air is a traditional one, probably 'Taymouth' which was also adapted by Sir Hugh.

Roamin' in the Gloamin'

Sir Harry Lauder

I've seen lots o' bonnie lassies trav'llin' far and wide,
But my heart is centred noo on bonnie Kate McBride.
And although I'm no' a chap that throws a word away,
I'm surprised mysel' sometimes at a' I've got to say.

Roamin' in the gloamin' on the bonnie banks o' Clyde,
Roamin' in the gloamin' wi' my lassie by my side,
When the sun has gone to rest,
That's the time that we love best,
O it's lovely roamin' in the gloamin'!

One nicht in the gloamin' we were trippin' side by side,
Kissed her twice, and asked her once if she would be my bride.
She was shy, so was I, we were baith the same,
But I got brave and braver, on the journey comin' hame.

Roamin' in the gloamin', etc.

Last nicht efter strollin' we got hame at half past nine,
Sittin' at the kitchen fire I asked her to be mine,
When she promised, I got up and danced the Hielan' fling
I've just been at the jew'ller's and I've picked a nice wee ring.

Roamin' in the gloamin', etc.

(*Spoken after third verse*)

Wait till I show you this nice wee ring!
(*Searching pockets.*) Surely I haven't lost it!
No! here it is. Man, when I think on sittin' at
the fire last nicht, and listenin' to the kettle singin' . . .

Roamin' in the gloamin', etc.

Reproduced by permission of Francis Day & Hunter Limited, 138–140 Charing Cross Road, London WC2

ROAMIN' IN THE GLOAMIN'
This song was written by the great Sir Harry Lauder and sung not only by him but by everyone who has come to the Bonny Banks O' Clyde for holidays.

The sun certainly has not set on the bonny banks, for the steamers still carry their happy cargoes of holiday-makers throughout the Scottish summers and the song is still sung with gusto.

Majestic Balmoral Castle, Aberdeenshire.

The Waggle O' The Kilt

Sir Harry Lauder

I'll never forget the day I went and join'd the 'Ninety third',
The chums I used to run with said they thought I look'd absurd,
They saluted me, and gather'd round me in a ring,
And as I wagg'd my tartan kilt they a' began to sing,

He's a braw braw Hielan' laddie,
Private Jack McDade.
There's not anither soger like him in the Scotch Brigade.
Rear'd amang the heather, you can see he's Scottish built
By the wig, wig, wiggle, wiggle, waggle o' the kilt.

I'll never forget the day we were order'd on review,
The King came down to see us, and the Queen was with him too,
As I march'd by the royal coach the King just shook his head,
The Queen put on her royal spec's and look'd at me and said,

He's a braw braw Hielan' laddie, etc.

I'll never forget the day we went away to camp.
The sun was hot, I drank a lot, I was nearly dead with cramp.
I'm very nearly certain sure I would have died that day,
But the thing that saved my life was when the band began to play,

He's a braw braw Hielan' laddie, etc.

Reproduced by permission of Francis Day & Hunter Limited, 138–140 Charing Cross Road, London WC2

THE WAGGLE O' THE KILT
One of the many 'hit' songs written by Sir Harry Lauder who knew more about waggling the kilt than most. It is, of course, a music-hall song with a great lilt to it and, if you sing it at the right tempo, you'll find that it keeps in time with any passing Highlander.
Not everyone smiles at the waggle of the kilt. The troops of Napoleon and, later, Kaiser Bill for example hardly had time to muster a smile before many of them died. But for now, let's smile again with Sir Harry Lauder.

Rothesay Bay

Dinah Maria Mulock and A. Scott-Gatty

Fu' yellow lie the corn rigs
Far down the braid hillside;
It is the brawest hairst field
Alang the shores o' Clyde,
And I'm a puir hairst lassie
Wha stands the lee lang day
Amang the corn rigs of Ardbeg
Abune sweet Rothesay Bay.

O I had ance a true love,
Now, I hae nane a va;
And I had three braw brithers,
But I hae tint them a;
My father and my mither sleep
I' the mools this day.
I sit my lane amang the rigs
Abune sweet Rothesay Bay.

It's a bonnie bay at morning,
And bonnier at the noon,
But bonniest when the sun draps
And red comes up the moon:
When the mist creeps o'er the Cumbrays,
And Arran peaks are grey,
And the great black hills,
Like sleepin' kings,
Sit grand roun' Rothesay Bay.

Then a bit sigh stirs my bosom,
And a wee tear blin's my ee,
And I think of that far countrie
Whar I wad like to be.
But I rise content i' the morning
To wark while wark I may
I' the yellow hairst field of Ardbeg
Abune sweet Rothesay Bay.

ROTHESAY BAY
The town of Rothesay on the Isle of Bute is the county town of Buteshire. It has long been a favourite holiday resort on the Firth of Clyde. Looking over its bay towards the Kyles of Bute, it contemplates the hills of Argyllshire – 'the great black hills like sleepin' kings'.

The castle, captured by the Norsemen in 1230, still keeps its drowsy guard over the island.

As a boy in Innellan, I used to gaze at sunny Rothesay on the other side of Loch Striven and can vouch for the description – 'sweet Rothesay Bay'.

The words of the song were written by Dinah Maria Mulock (1826–87), the author of John Halifax, Gentleman *and the attractive melody by Alfred Scott-Gatty the composer of operettas.*

The Road to the Isles

K. MacLeod

A far croonin' is pullin' me away
As take I wi' my cromak to the road,
The far Coolins are puttin' love on me
As step I wi' the sunlight for my load.

Sure, by Tummel and Loch Rannoch and Lochaber I will go,
By heather tracks wi' heaven in their wiles;
If it's thinkin' in your inner heart braggart's in my step,
You've never smelt the tangle o' the Isles.
Oh, the far Coolins are putting' love on me,
As step I wi' my cromak to the Isles.

It's by Sheil water the track is to the west,
By Aillort and by Morar to the sea,
The cool cresses I am thinkin' o' for pluck,
And bracken for a wink on Mother knee.

Sure, by Tummel and Loch Rannoch and Lochaber I will go, etc.

It's the blue Islands are pullin' me away,
Their laughter puts the leap upon the lame,
The blue Islands from the Skerries to the Lews,
Wi' heather honey taste upon each name.

Sure, by Tummel and Loch Rannoch and Lochaber I will go, etc.

Reprinted from Songs of the Hebrides *by permission of the Trustees of the Estate of Marjory Kennedy-Fraser and Boosey & Hawkes, Music Publishers Limited*

THE ROAD TO THE ISLES
Here is a song known in every part of the world. When I pass through any of the places mentioned in it, I, like most others begin to sing to myself these well-loved words.

The air was taken down from the chanter-playing of Malcolm Johnson and arranged by Patuffa Kennedy-Fraser. The memorable words were written by Kenneth MacLeod, the Gaelic scholar of Gigha.

The Cuillin Hills of Skye are putting their mystic spell on the writer who is resolved to go to them along the course of the River Tummel, by the banks of Loch Rannoch and by the Braes of Lochaber. Glen Shiel will take him, like its river, to the sea, but he will be tramping instead over the hills to Loch Aillort and Morar where at last will be the Atlantic, the pathway to his goal.

Stretched before him are 'the blue Islands from the Skerries to the Lews' but best of all, he will behold the island called by Norsemen 'the Winged Isle', and by Ossian 'the Isle of Mist' – the island of Skye!

There are many different roads to the Isles but there is only one such song and it, like the journey it describes, is a great one!

Loch Tummel, Perthshire.

The Corran Narrows, Inverness-shire.

The Mingulay Boat Song

Anonymous

Chorus

Hill you ho, boys;
Let her go, boys;
Bring her head round,
Now all together.
Hill you ho, boys;
Let her go, boys;
Sailing home,
Home to Mingulay.

What care we though white the Minch is?
What care we for wind or weather?
Let her go, boys!
Ev'ry inch is wearing home,
Home to Mingulay.

Hill you ho, boys; etc.

Wives are waiting on the bank,
Or looking seaward from the heather;
Pull her round boys!
And we'll anchor,
Ere the sun sets at Mingulay.

Hill you ho, boys; etc.

Reproduced by kind permission of Roberton Publications

THE MINGULAY BOAT SONG
Mingulay is virtually the southernmost island in the Outer Hebrides.
Since the principal occupation there is fishing, the surrounding Atlantic is regarded as a Great Provider. It is also the way of the parting and the way of the homecoming. There is a swing to the song which is the swing of strong men rowing their boat towards a happy reunion at the quayside.

Sunset over Luing from Arduaine, Argyllshire.

The Song of the Clyde

R. Y. Bell and I. Gourlay

I sing of a river I'm happy beside,
The song that I sing is a song of the Clyde.
Of all Scottish rivers it's dearest to me,
It flows from Leadhills all the way to the sea.
It borders the orchards of Lanark so fair;
Meanders through meadows with sheep grazing there:
But from Glasgow to Greenock, in towns on each side,
The hammers' ding-dong is the song of the Clyde.

Oh the River Clyde, the wonderful Clyde!
The name of it thrills me and fills me with pride,
And I'm satisfied, whate'er may betide,
The sweetest of songs is the song of the Clyde.

Imagine we've left Craigendoran behind,
And wind-happy yachts by Kilcreggan we find;
At Kirn and Dunoon and Innellan we stay;
Then Scotland's Madeira that's Rothesay, they say.
Or maybe by Fairlie and Largs we will go;
Or over to Millport that thrills people so;
Maybe journey to Arran it can't be denied,
Those scenes all belong to the song of the Clyde.

Oh the River Clyde, the wonderful Clyde!, etc.

When sun sets on dockland, there's beauty to see.
The cry of a seabird is music to me.
The blast of a horn loudly echoes, and then
A stillness descends on the water again.
'Tis here that the sea-going liners are born:
But, unlike the salmon, they seldom return.
Can you wonder the Scots o'er the ocean so wide,
Should constantly long for the song of the Clyde?

Oh the River Clyde, the wonderful Clyde!, etc.

Optional patter verse

There's Paw an' Maw at Glasgow Broomielaw;
They're goin' doon the water for 'The Fair'.
There's Bob an' Mary, on the Govan Ferry,
Wishin' jet propulsion could be there.
There's steamers cruisin', and there's 'buddies' snoozin',
And there's laddies fishin' frae the pier;
An' Paw's perspirin', very near expirin',
As he rows a boat frae there to here.
With eyes aflashin', it is voted smashin',
To be walkin' daily on the prom:
And May and Evelyn are in seventh heaven
As they stroll along with Dick and Tom.
And Dumbarton Rock to ev'ry Jean and Jock,
Extends a welcome that is high and wide:
Seems to know that they are on their homeward way
To hear the song of the Clyde.

Oh the River Clyde, the wonderful Clyde!, etc.

Reproduced by kind permission of Kerr Music and Bayley & Ferguson Limited

THE SONG OF THE CLYDE
Written by R. Y. Bell and Ian Gourlay, this song became one of the most popular songs to come out of Scotland in post-war years.

'Paw and Maw' and the 'weans' have been a celebrated part of holidays 'doon the watter' for many a long year and one of the great attractions of the song is its mention of all the favourite resorts on the Clyde, each with its steadfast multitude of devotees.

The melody too is catchy and easily mastered even by the most 'timmer-tuned'.

Corn Rigs Are Bonnie

Robert Burns

It was upon a Lammas night,
When corn rigs are bonnie,
Beneath the moon's unclouded light
I held awa to Annie:
The time flew by wi' tentless heed,
Till 'tween the late and early,
Wi' sma' persuasion she agreed
To see me thro' the barley.

Corn rigs, an' barley rigs,
Corn rigs are bonnie,
I'll ne'er forget that happy night,
Amang the rigs wi' Annie.

The sky was blue, the wind was still,
The moon was shining clearly;
I set her down wi' right good will
Amang the rigs o' barley.
I kent her heart was a' my ain;
I lov'd her most sincerely;
I kiss'd her owre and owre again
Amang the rigs o' barley.

Corn rigs, etc.

I lock'd her in my fond embrace,
Her heart was beating rarely;
My blessing on that happy place,
Amang the rigs o' barley!
But by the moon and stars so bright,
That shone that hour so clearly,
She aye shall bless that happy night,
Amang the rigs o' barley.

Corn rigs, etc.

I hae been blythe wi' comrades dear,
I hae been merry drinkin';
I hae been joyfu' gath'rin' gear,
I hae been happy thinkin';
But a' the pleasures e'er I saw,
Tho' three times doubled fairly,
That happy night was worth them a',
Amang the rigs o' barley.

Corn rigs, etc.

Reproduced by kind permission of Kerr Music and Bayley & Ferguson Limited

CORN RIGS ARE BONNIE
One of the earliest poetic efforts of Robert Burns and said to have been inspired either by Annie Ronald or Annie Blair, both of whom lived locally.

The original words were somewhat less genteel than those which Burns eventually produced.

The air is of English origin, composed in 1680 to a song by D'Urfey, beginning 'Sawney was tall and of noble race'. It was used later by Alan Ramsey in 1725 and by John Gay in 1729.

The corn rigs are still in abundance in Ayrshire and continue to serve the amorous role allotted them by Burns.

Méaveg and Loch Ceann Dibig, Harris, Outer Hebrides.

An Eriskay Love Lilt

Adapted by Marjory Kennedy-Fraser and K. MacLeod

Chorus
Vair me o ro van o,
Vair me o ro van ee,
Vair me o ru o ho,
Sad am I without thee.

When I'm lonely dear white heart,
Black the night or wild the sea,
By love's light my foot finds,
The old pathway to thee.

Vair me o ro van o, etc.

Thou'rt the music of my heart,
Harp of joy, oh cruit mo chridh,*
Moon of guidance by night,
Strength and light thou'rt to me.

Vair me o ro van o, etc.

* Means 'harp of my heart' and is pronounced 'crootch mo chree'.

Reprinted from Songs of the Hebrides *by permission of the Trustees of the Estate of Marjory Kennedy-Fraser and Boosey & Hawkes, Music Publishers Limited*

AN ERISKAY LOVE LILT

The island of Eriskay lies between Barra and South Uist in the Outer Hebrides. It is only three miles long by one and a half miles across. It is rocky and poorly blessed with soil but like its small population it has great charm, a rich history of Gaelic music and believe it or not – a football-field!

It was on this small island that Prince Charles Edward Stewart first set foot on Scottish soil at the beginning of his Rising in 1745 and the bay where he landed is still called Prince's Bay.

But today the main fame of the island rests on this song which was first heard from the lips of Mary Macinnes of Eriskay. It has been translated into countless languages and sung by countless voices. Its plaintive beauty seems to me to capture the whole enchantment of the Hebrides.

The Northern Lights of Old Aberdeen

Mary Webb

When I was a lad, a tiny wee lad
My mother said to me,
'Come see the Northern Lights my boy
They're bright as they can be.'
She called them the heavenly dancers,
Merry dancers in the sky.
I'll never forget that wonderful sight,
They made the heavens bright.

The Northern Lights of Old Aberdeen
Mean Home Sweet Home to me.
The Northern Lights of Aberdeen.
Are what I long to see.
I've been a wand'rer all of my life
And many a sight I've seen,
God speed the day when I'm on my way
To my home in Aberdeen.

I've wandered in many far-off lands,
And travelled many a mile.
I've missed the folk I've cherished most,
The joy of a friendly smile.
It warms up the heart of the wand'rer,
The clasp of a welcoming hand,
To greet me when I return,
Home to my native land.

The Northern Lights of Old Aberdeen, etc.

Reproduced by kind permission of Kerr Music and Bayley & Ferguson Limited

THE NORTHERN LIGHTS OF OLD ABERDEEN
Every Aberdonian has at some time seen the Aurora Borealis or Northern Lights above his city.

They are seen only in and towards Polar regions but I doubt very much if anyone from Aberdeen would admit to living anywhere near the North Pole.

The song by Mary Webb refers to 'the heavenly dancers' but to many a fisherman returning with his catch to Aberdeen Harbour, the 'northern lights' he has in mind are those of the Granite City herself.

The Uist Tramping Song (Come Along)

Sir Hugh Roberton

Chorus
Come along, come along,
Let us foot it out together;
Come along, come along,
Be it fair or stormy weather,
With the hills of home before us
And the purple of the heather,
Let us sing in happy chorus,
Come along, come along!

So gaily sings the lark,
And the sky's all awake,
With the promise of the day,
For the road we gladly take;
So it's heel and toe and forward,
Bidding farewell to the town,
For the welcome that awaits us
Ere the sun goes down.

Come along, come along, etc.

It's the call of sea and shore,
It's the tang of bog and peat,
And the scent of brier and myrtle
That puts magic in our feet;
So it's on we go rejoicing,
Over bracken, over stile;
And it's soon we will be tramping
Out the last long mile.

Come along, come along, etc.

Reproduced by kind permission of Roberton Publications

THE UIST TRAMPING SONG
The islands of North and South Uist belong to the chain of the islands of the Outer Hebrides, known collectively as the 'Long Island'.

This song, written by Sir Hugh Roberton, gives the true feeling engendered by the Uists. They are a paradise for holiday-makers especially if they are keen on walking and fishing. In South Uist alone there are one hundred and ninety freshwater lochs, some of them filled with the finest brown trout in the British Isles.

So get your fishing-rod and 'let us foot it out together'.

Invercauld House, Morayshire.

Lagganulva and Laggan Bay, Isle of Mull.

Aignish on the Machair (Going West)

Agnes Mure Mackenzie

When day and night are over,
And the world is done with me,
Oh carry me West and lay me
In Aignish, Aignish by the sea.

And never heed me lying
Among the ancient dead,
Beside the white sea breakers
And sand-drift overhead.
The grey gulls wheeling ever,
And the wide arch of sky,
Oh Aignish, Aignish on the Machair,
And quiet, quiet there to lie.
And quiet, quiet there to lie.

Reprinted from Songs of the Hebrides *by permission of the Trustees of the Estate of Marjory Kennedy-Fraser and Boosey & Hawkes, Music Publishers Limited*

AIGNISH ON THE MACHAIR
The words to this song are by Agnes Mure Mackenzie of Stornoway, Lewis and the air is old Highland.

The 'machair' is the grassland that covers the wide sandy plain along the shore of the Atlantic through all the Outer Hebrides. On it are wild flowers and above it the song of the skylark and the call of the lapwing.

If it's quietness you are looking for and a place where a man can be alone with his thoughts, then you'll go down to the machair with the sea for a friend, the silver sand under foot and the blue island sky to cover your head. There you can think the thoughts of life itself and maybe what comes after.

George Square, Glasgow.

The Royal Mile

K. McKellar and I. Gourlay

If fate decreed that I could walk but just one mile each day,
And I with age and sorrows weighed were giv'n my choice of way.
I'd choose from ev'ry mile I've crossed on land or sea or air.
The mile that makes a Scotsman proud of Edinburgh fair.

O let me walk the Royal Mile, that's Scotland's brave highway;
Where at one o'clock from the Castle Rock comes 'Auld Reekie's' call each day,
And as the echo sounds in the Palace grounds,
Then the Heav'ns on Scotland smile,
And you've made your day in a royal way on the Royal Mile,
Yes you've made your day in a royal way on the Royal Mile.

When I walked this famous mile the air about me rings
With footsteps made in years gone by by princes, queens and kings.
For here is Scotland's history, here freedom lost and won,
And here my heart is ever homing, 'til my life is done.

O let me walk the Royal Mile, etc.

Reproduced by permission of Francis Day & Hunter Limited, 138–140 Charing Cross Road, London WC2

THE ROYAL MILE
These words I wrote to be included in an historical scena at the Alhambra Theatre in Glasgow.

The Royal Mile was the scene of the passage of Prince Charlie first in glory and later in defeat. It saw Mary Queen of Scots as the darling of the Capital and subsequently as its prisoner. It rang to the hue and cry of the followers of William Wallace and resounded to the determined tread of John Knox. Bothwell caroused here; Rizzio was murdered a dagger's throw from it.

Nowadays, the only awesome sound to be heard is the clicking of tourists' cameras, relentlessly capturing square inches of history!

The melody was composed by my friend, Ian Gourlay.

Kelvin Grove

Anonymous

Let us haste to Kelvin Grove, bonnie lassie, O,
Through its mazes let us rove, bonnie lassie, O,
Where the roses in their pride
Deck the bonnie dingle side,
Where the midnight fairies glide, bonnie lassie, O.

Let us wander by the mill, bonnie lassie, O,
To the cove beside the rill, bonnie lassie, O,
Where the glens rebound the call
Of the roaring waters' fall
Through the mountain's rocky hall, bonnie lassie, O.

O Kelvin banks are fair, bonnie lassie, O,
When the summer we are there, bonnie lassie, O,
There the May-pink crimson plume
Throws a soft but sweet perfume
Round the yellow banks of broom, bonnie lassie, O.

Though I dare not call thee mine, bonnie lassie, O,
As the smile of fortune's thine, bonnie lassie, O,
Yet with fortune on my side
I could stay thy father's pride,
And win thee for my bride, bonnie lassie, O.

But the frowns of fortune lour, bonnie lassie, O,
On thy lover at this hour, bonnie lassie, O,
Ere yon golden orb of day,
Wake the warblers on the spray,
From this land I must away, bonnie lassie, O.

Then farewell to Kelvin Grove, bonnie lassie, O,
And adieu to all I love, bonnie lassie, O,
To the river winding clear,
To the fragrant scented brier,
Even to thee of all most dear, bonnie lassie, O.

When upon a foreign shore, bonnie lassie, O,
Should I fall midst battle's roar, bonnie lassie, O,
Then, Helen! shouldst thou hear,
Of thy lover on his bier,
To his memory shed a tear, bonnie lassie, O.

KELVIN GROVE
'Kelvin Grove, a picturesque and richly wooded dell, through which the river Kelvin flows, lies a very distance to the North-West of Glasgow and will in all probability soon be comprehended within the wide-spreading boundaries of the city itself.' These words were written in 1853 and the prediction contained in them has indeed come true. Kelvin Grove has been engulfed by twentieth-century Glasgow and near by stands the Broadcasting House of the B.B.C.

Thankfully, however, it is still a little beauty-spot and perhaps even more warmly appreciated than of yore.

The Sound of Sleat from the Isle of Skye.

The Skye Boat Song

Sir Harold Boulton

Chorus

Speed bonnie boat like a bird on the wing,
'Onward' the sailors cry,
Carry the lad that's born to be King
Over the sea to Skye.

Loud the winds howl,
Loud the waves roar,
Thunderclaps rend the air,
Baffled, our foes
Stand by the shore,
Follow they will not dare.

Speed bonnie boat like a bird on the wing, etc.

Though the waves leap,
Soft shall ye sleep,
Ocean's a royal bed,
Rocked in the deep
Flora will keep
Watch o'er your weary head.

Speed bonnie boat like a bird on the wing, etc.

Many's the man
Fought on that day,
Well the claymore could wield,
When the night came
Silently lay
Dead on Culloden's field.

Speed bonnie boat like a bird on the wing, etc.

Burned are our homes,
Exile and death
Scattered the loyal men,
Yet ere the sword
Cool in the sheath
Charlie will come again

Speed bonnie boat like a bird on the wing, etc.

THE SKYE BOAT SONG
It was by boat from Uist to the island of Skye that Flora Macdonald took Bonnie Prince Charlie after his defeat at the Battle of Culloden. He was disguised as her serving-maid.

The romance, if any, which was popularly supposed to have existed between them could at any rate not have been a lasting one, for four years after Prince Charlie had fled from Scotland Flora married her clansman, Macdonald of Kingsburgh.

Flora survived the exiled Prince by two years and, dying at the age of sixty-eight, was buried in the old churchyard of Kilmuir in Skye.

'The lad that was born to be King' lies buried near his birthplace in Rome.

The Lewis Bridal Song (Mairi's Wedding)

Adapted by Sir Hugh Roberton

Chorus
Step we gaily, on we go,
Heel for heel and toe for toe,
Arm in arm and row on row,
All for Mairi's wedding.

Over hillways up and down,
Myrtle green and bracken brown,
Past the shielings, thro' the town;
All for sake o' Mairi.

Step we gaily, on we go, etc.

Red her cheeks as rowans are,
Bright her eye as any star,
Fairest o' them a' by far,
Is our darling Mairi.

Step we gaily, on we go, etc.

Plenty herring, plenty meal,
Plenty peat to fill her creel,
Plenty bonnie bairns as weel;
That's the toast for Mairi.

Step we gaily, on we go, etc.

Reproduced by kind permission of Roberton Publications

THE LEWIS BRIDAL SONG
'The Lewis Bridal Song' as shown here was adapted by Sir Hugh Roberton from an earlier song of the same name.

I have been at a wedding on the island of Lewis and, although I stayed for a mere hour and a half, the reception continued for five days and five nights with the bride and bridegroom in attendance throughout. It seems that nothing is hurried in Lewis! Except perhaps the progress of the guests towards such a wedding-reception!

The Peat-Fire Flame

K. MacLeod

Far away and o'er the moor,
Far away and o'er the moor,
Morar waits for a boat that saileth,
Far away down Lowland way,
I dream the dream I learned, lad,
By the light o' the peat-fire flame,
Light for love, for lilt o' grail-deeds.
By the light o' the peat-fire flame,
The light the hill-folk yearn for.

Far away, down Lowland way,
Far away, down Lowland way,
Grim's the toil, without tune or dream, lad,
All you need's a creel and love
For the dream the heart can weave, lad,
By the light of the peat-fire flame,
Light for love, for lilt, for laughter,
By the light o' the peat-fire flame,
The light the hill-folk yearn for.

Far away and o'er the moor,
Far away the tramp and tread,
Tune and laughter of all the heroes,
Pulls me onward o'er the trail
Of the dream my heart may weave, lad,
By the light of the peat-fire flame,
Light for love, for lilt, for laughter,*
By the light of the peat-fire flame,
The light the hill-folk yearn for.

* Alternatively – 'Light for love, for lilt o' grail-deeds'.

Reprinted from Songs of the Hebrides *by permission of the Trustees of the Estate of Marjory Kennedy-Fraser and Boosey & Hawkes, Music Publishers Limited*

THE PEAT-FIRE FLAME
This is described by Marjory Kennedy-Fraser as a tramping song and a companion to 'The Road to the Isles'. The tune was played on a chanter by Malcolm Johnson to Kenneth MacLeod, the Gaelic Editor of the celebrated collection Songs of the Hebrides. *Kenneth MacLeod wrote the words shown here.*

The peat fire is to this day the sole means of heating many houses in the Hebrides where a peat-bog is more easily accessible than a coal-field in Lanarkshire.

Rodel Church, Harris, Outer Hebrides.

Loch of the Lowes, Selkirkshire.

The Flowers of the Forest

Jean Elliot

I've heard them lilting at our yowe-milking,
Lasses a-lilting before the dawn o' day;
But now they are moaning on ilka green loaning,
'The Flowers of the Forest are a' wede away.'

At buchts in the morning, nae blythe lads are scorning,
The lasses are lonely, and dowie, and wae;
Nae daffin', nae gabbin', but sighing and sabbing:
Ilk ane lifts her leglin, and hies her away.

In hairst, at the shearing, nae youths now are jeering,
The bandsters are lyart, and runkled and grey;
At fair or at preaching, nae wooing, nae fleeching:
The Flowers of the Forest are a' wede away.

At e'en, in the gloaming, nae swankies are roaming
'Bout stacks wi' the lasses at bogle to play,
But ilk ane sits drearie, lamenting her dearie:
The Flowers of the Forest are a' wede away.

Dule and wae for the order, sent our lads to the Border!
The English for ance, by guile wan the day;
The Flowers of the Forest, that foucht aye the foremost,
The prime o' our land, are cauld in the clay.

We'll hear nae mair lilting at our yowe-milking,
Women and bairns are heartless and wae;
Sighing and moaning on ilka green loaning:
'The Flowers of the Forest are a' wede away.'

Reproduced by kind permission of Kerr Music and Bayley & Ferguson Limited

THE FLOWERS OF THE FOREST
The Battle of Flodden was fought on 9 September 1513. During it, King James IV of Scotland and the flower of his nobility were slain.

The forest referred to in the title is the district in Scotland anciently and sometimes still called 'The Forest' which embraces the whole of Selkirkshire, a portion of Peeblesshire and even part of Clydesdale. It was a favourite resort of Scottish Kings and nobles for hunting.

The words were written by a Miss Jean Elliot (1727–1805) who published them anonymously but whose identity was soon discovered by Sir Walter Scott among others.

Loch Shiel and the Glenfinnan Monument.

Will Ye No Come Back Again?

Lady Nairne

Royal Charlie's now awa',
Safely owre the friendly main;
Mony a heart will break in twa,
Should he ne'er come back again.

Will ye no come back again?
Will ye no come back again?
Better lo'ed ye canna be,
Will ye no come back again?

Mony a traitor 'mang the Isles,
Brak' the band o' nature's law;
Mony a traitor wi' his wiles,
Sought to wear his life awa'.

Will ye no come back again?, etc.

Ye trusted in your Hieland men,
They trusted you dear Charlie,
They kent your hiding in the glen,
Death or exile braving.

Will ye no come back again?, etc.

We watched thee in the gloaming hour,
We watched thee in the morning grey,
Tho' thirthy thousand pounds they'd gie,
Oh! there is none that would betray.

Will ye no come back again?, etc.

The hills he trode were a' his ain,
And bed beneath the birken trees;
The bush that hid him on the plain,
There's none on earth can claim but he.

Will ye no come back again?, etc.

Whene'er I hear the blackbird sing,
Unto the e'ening sinkin' doun,
Or merle that mak's the woods to ring,
To me they hae nae ither soun'!

Will ye no come back again?, etc.

Mony a gallant sodjer fought,
Mony a gallant chief did fa',
Death itself were dearly bought,
A' for Scotland's King and law.

Will ye no come back again?, etc.

Sweet the lav'rocks note and lang,
Liltin' wildly up the glen;
And aye to me he sings ae song,
'Will ye no come back again?'

Will ye no come back again?, etc.

Reproduced by kind permission of Kerr Music and Bayley & Ferguson Limited

WILL YE NO COME BACK AGAIN?
This haunting song was written by Lady Nairne, a poetess steeped in the lore of the Jacobite Rising.

When Prince Charles had landed on the coast of Moidart in 1745, he was the embodiment of hope, kingliness and manly beauty. Fourteen months later he shrank into the rescuing French ship in a state of heart-broken squalor and degradation. Did he in fact come back again? It was believed widely that he did come back in 1750 and 1753. No less a person than Sir Walter Scott introduced him into his novel Redgauntlet *in the character of Father Buonaventure, the 'Royal Wanderer'. So far the question implicit in the song has remained unanswered.*

Auld Lang Syne

Robert Burns

Should auld acquaintance be forgot,
And never brought to min'?
Should auld acquaintance be forgot,
And days of lang syne?

For auld lang syne, my dear,
For auld lang syne,
We'll tak' a cup o' kindness yet,
For auld lang syne.

We twa hae run about the braes,
And pu'd the gowans fine;
But we've wander'd mony a weary foot,
Sin' auld lang syne.

For auld lang syne, my dear, etc.

We twa hae paidled i' the burn,
Frae morning sun till dine;
But seas between us braid hae roar'd
Sin' auld lang syne.

For auld lang syne, my dear, etc.

And there's a hand, my trusty fiere,
And gie's a hand o' thine;
And we'll tak' a right gude-willy waught,
For auld lang syne.

For auld lang syne, my dear, etc.

And surely ye'll be your pint-stowp,
And surely I'll be mine!
And we'll tak' a cup o' kindness yet,
For auld lang syne.

For auld lang syne, my dear, etc.

Reproduced by kind permission of Kerr Music and Bayley & Ferguson Limited

AULD LANG SYNE
The second and third verses of 'Auld Lang Syne' are by Robert Burns; the others, as he himself indicated, are old.

He remarked of the original verses that 'this old song of the olden times' had never been in print nor even in manuscript until he took it down from an old man's singing.

The verses were later set to the pentatonic air, 'I fee'd a lad at Michaelmas', since which time the song has been regarded as a Scottish National Anthem.

No gathering of friends is properly concluded without the song being sung and no social occasion is more honoured than when the singers have taken the trouble to learn the correct words! Such an opportunity is now offered to the reader.

The Palnure Burn in Glen Trool National Forest Park.

Other titles on Scotland by Jarrold Colour Publications, Norwich

COLOUR BOOK SERIES: *Colourful Scotland (bound)* COTMAN HOUSE SERIES: *Bonnie Prince Charlie Country · Robert Burns' Scotland* SANDRINGHAM SERIES: *Scotland · Scottish Highlands* COTMAN COLOR SERIES: *Loch Leven & Glencoe · Argyllshire · Around the Cairngorms · Balmoral Countryside · Bonnie Scotland · Castles of Scotland · Edinburgh · Firth of Clyde · Heart of the Highlands · Inverness-shire · Isle of Skye · Loch Lomond & The Trossachs · Lochs of Scotland · Perthshire · Ross & Cromarty · Scott Country · Sutherland & Caithness · Western Highlands* TOURIST GUIDE: *Your Holiday in Scotland*